# UNREST

23 New & 45 Present Past Poems

# UNREST

## 23 New & 45 Present Past Poems

## Emily Fragos

The Sheep Meadow Press

Rhinebeck, New York

Designed and typeset by The Sheep Meadow Press.
Distributed by Syracuse University Press

All inquiries and permission requests should be addressed
to the publisher:

The Sheep Meadow Press
P.O. Box 84
Rhinebeck, NY 12572

Names: Fragos, Emily, author.
Title: Unrest : 23 new & 45 present past poems / Emily Fragos.
Description: Rhinebeck, New York : The Sheep Meadow Press, [2021] |
Identifiers: LCCN 2021019116 | ISBN 978-1-937679-94-1 (paperback)
Subjects: LCGFT: Poetry.
Classification: LCC PS3606.R345 U57 2021 | DDC 811/.6--dc23
LC record available at https://lccn.loc.gov/2021019116

Cover Art:  LERA AUERBACH, © *Eve's Lament,* mixed media, kind courtesy of Lera Auerbach.

Author Photograph:  YUKA URUSHIBATA

For my dear friends
for their love and support
for their great kindness

# Contents

**Selected Poems from Hostage**

*If you want to understand someone's heart*
*find out what breaks it.*
Stanley Moss

# New Poems

*Trumpet*

I admit it, my life, I was totally taken with you. I went along,
laughing and smiling, or sometimes on the verge of tears, good god,
groveling in the halls for your praise and recognition,
your adoration. Meanwhile, bodies mean nothing, you said.

You think yours is so special, you laughed. The deserts are strewn
with them. Graves, pits, rivers are jam-packed with bodies, you said.
But the music was cathartic, I said, the glorious waves of sound.
Don't you remember the jazz trumpeter in Paris,

how I rode behind him on his hog on the Champs-Élysées
in the middle of the night. I held on for dear life. Ha!
Don't let me stop you, you said. Apricot jam on fresh croissants
and the little room, the bed with bright white sheets,

the window overlooking the park . . .
Everyone's Paris memory, you said, with a yawn.
I'm gonna play the trumpet 'til I'm not here anymore,
jazzman crooned.  Me, too, I said, whirling like a dervish in

that *chambre de bonne,* I want to live like *that,* with my heart
swelling, my whole body alive and spinning and thrilling for you,
my life. We held hands, we jumped up and down, we screamed . . .
What more do you want from me, you said.

*The Dream Called Us*
> *...le rêve qu'on appelle nous* – Tristan Tzara

At noon the deranged one feels his ravaged mind
Going away from him like his mother.
A long-haired figure in dirty clothes,

He stands beneath Beethoven's window and listens,
His brown eyes filling with tears.
Prowling the cobblestone streets, he trips and goes

Flying, a floating form in a sunken ship,
His head softly bumping against the invisible hull.
"I am a scarecrow in a field of crows,"

He repeats to himself. "I can never go to sleep."
Into the mound of trash, he plunges his hands
Where broken-stemmed lilies and hydrangeas bloom

Amid orange peels and fish scales.
I do not know what came next and next
In this young man's life. Heard centuries later,

His story has faded as all stories do--beginnings
That never end. Glimpsed from the dusty window
Of a passing train, there is a donkey in the distance

By a lopsided fence, his old tail hanging down
Like a useless, frayed rope, his hide of purple sores.
A man is moving toward him with something in his hand.

## A Quiet Evening

In the square, white building with one light burning,
a woman sorts laundry into cardboard boxes.

A mute servant brings goblets of wine
for the groom and his child bride.

She is sinking so deeply into silence
as he caresses her face,

she may never speak again.
Everything about her

has just ended.
A fortune-teller plays cards with herself.

She shoves her swollen feet into soft, pink slippers,
her life's grand pleasure.

Trudging along the train tracks after midnight,
the circus elephants know the way. The leader's trunk

curls like a periscope around each corner and her meek
brethren follow, holding each other by the tail.

*The Competition*

I have a wound to the hip and a wound to the heart, I said to the boardwalk fortune-teller. Which one do you suffer, she asked me, body or spirit, for there can only be one pain. Those who are starving eat the bark of trees, she explained, for hunger is the pain and none other. The heart goes numb. Choose your fortune, she said, $6 for one palm or $10 for both. But that is so primitive, I said, surprised at my confidence in the face of authority. The heart hungers, too, I said, for the hunger of the heart is passion. Never have I felt so alive, so inspired, as when I have hungered with the heart. Everything is surely connected. Madame Athena, as she billed herself, shifted in her seat. The aura is departing, she sighed, I cannot read you. I left her little booth in sadness and confusion. I hardly noticed the usual suspects of a winter boardwalk, the homeless on their benches, the stray dogs, the squawking gulls, the empty, eerie arcade. You can come back, Madame Athena said, placing her bejeweled hand upon mine, when, like water, you are poured out.

*You Have Devoured Everything*

You have devoured everything.
The walls have caved in, the house is in rubble.
I walk the streets, nothingness spreads

the invisible ink inside of me.
What if, what if, I sob like the inconsolable child
I have become, my head in the stone lion's lap.

Where are you now, donning your face
and flowing gown, your smile for the lover
who leaves his scent upon the soft portals of your body.

*The Suicide of Cesare Pavese*

a buried child
come unearthed

a zero sum
a gaping hole

there all along
one step ahead

and fallen into
mid-sentence

he imagined her naked
in his big bed at night

her body wreathing
and warm against his

he imagined her face
with the man she was really with

stop it make it stop
slow and silent

as a starving animal
at a roadside zoo

as a broken-stemmed flower
no one but you no one

*Unrest*

At the shelter, the cats are kept in glass-enclosed cases with just enough room to stand, walk a few steps and eat; but strangers come on weekends to adopt them, take them to larger rooms and give them new names: James, Tabitha, Snowball, Molière, so you would never know how they began their lives, in abuse, grave hunger, and deprivation, or what strange turbulence lies coiled up inside their bodies, as they float to the top of warm stone walls or sleep in a lone patch of sun on the newlyweds' bed.

*The Universe of Poetry*

death's no red plumed steed breaking down the door
death's no fantasy trip to planet your anus
death's  a dumb mushroom growing inside your head
death's hard to sleep and hard to breathe
death's the light switch in the basement going off
you've had your turn in the sun and the moon
so shove over, honeybunch, make room
for the new trumpet player on the block
life goes on, the forests and farms are teeming with life and

if you could go like that why should I worry about
I'm done with grieving for the lost the lonely the diseased
the old in their overcoats and big sneakers
the sick cats shitting outside the litter box
the lame dogs being pulled in their little red wagons
hold them up for as long as you can
then make that call for the final appointment
if you could go like that in a blink with no warning then it does not
in total confusion irate as I was I woke to the call

hand me that cigarette and match, turn on the TV
crime shows where maniacs strangle women with wire
comedies with laughter in a can
porn with tons of dumb fucking
I'm as gutless as a bomb, I'm as soulless as a shark
I'm as corny as Kansas in August
you blew me out of the water, girl
what could death possibly mean to me now
*Father says it's pretty much all real life*

Final line from <u>The</u> <u>Letters</u> <u>of</u> <u>Emily</u> <u>Dickinson</u>.

## A Space Where Anything Can Happen

A door opens in a Paris back street.
You see them dancing slowly with such dignity
and formality as if this were the end of the world

and the very last dance ever danced. One of the men
turns and looks back at you, without expression,
but you are eavesdropping on intimacy,

a silly, peeping person still among the living,
the squabbling,  the furiously unspooling.
You study the naked warrior who stands

cold and shattered in a corner of the gallery.
 You move up close to him and hear his rasp.
"I fed deer out of my hand. I plunged

my spear into the enemy's heart. A horse flew by
and my body went away from me. How can it be
I no longer exist. Stop staring at my dick!"

In a *chambre de bonne*, a young woman is
bathing herself. You see her pale back bend
by the open window. You watch as her arms

rise and float and reach for something
that must absolutely be totally exquisite.
There can be no such thing as usual.

## Taming the Parakeet

They are clever, inquisitive little birds who enjoy attention and praise. If you would like to tame your feathered friend and teach her a few tricks, you must first gain her trust. Then she will look forward to spending time with you. Items you will need: a tiny bell, water, seed, an assortment of colorful, plumed toys. Now, be humanly patient, for she comes to you from another world where stiff feathers cover skin; she has a hard beak, not soft lips, and feet like twigs, a perfect example of form following function. She does not seem to grow weary of her brief existence, not even caged, although when sleeping you can almost notice an Albrecht Dürer-like melancholia pass over her walnut face. At night she sleeps covered up like us. She clutches her perch and pecks at her food, delicately sipping water from a tiny glass bowl which I find so beautiful I could cry.

*Nihil*

You lived on nothing, on air.
It's no wonder you feed the birds
that come flying to you, the dog that runs
to get that liver treat in your hand.
No wonder you want to hug too tight and kiss
for the simplest gift. You are like the refugee
who cannot stop staring at the feast on the table,
the honeyed yams, the cherry pies. You live
as if released from prison after many years,
not guilty of any crime, misidentified.
No wonder you need to be left all alone,
as the long day follows after and the shock
pours into you, out of you, into you . . .

## Mercy

We are waiting by the door. We are waiting in the hospital's
little waiting room. We are waiting while the sun comes up
and goes back down, while the moon appears
and wanes. There are deep human prints
on the moon, are there not. They remain
in the fine, gray dust. Well, that is what we want.
The Buddha, the Jesus,
yammering pundits with all the answers,
teach us to see in this dark theater
when the radiant dancers have all gone home.
Teach us to breathe in magnificent desolation.
We are pulling out all the flower and leaving the stem bare.

*You and You*

Even if we cannot bear the thought of your warm
human touch, so painful to our mournful delicacy,

even if we do not hunger as you, we'd be grateful
for a glimpse, however fleeting. We'd stare at you

and you with frozen eyes, lips parted, as if we could
almost sing, feel almost what it felt like again.

## Little Fugue

I keep thinking today is Friday. The weather report was fair and mild. I went to the supermarket and the pharmacy. I encountered no hassle. Everything went according to plan. I bought the cat her food.

I keep thinking today is yesterday. Everything was fine, fine. I keep thinking nothing is horribly wrong. The cat is asleep in her basket, the TV is glowing, my head on the pillow.

My body will carry me through with a minimum of fuss, I keep thinking, my head on the pillow, I'll make amends, my conscience is clear.

My head on the pillow, the cat asleep, her favorite food. I keep thinking today is Friday and I am calm which is a beautiful thing. I accept everything that happens like a small animal.

Everyone has a plan, until they get hit. Mike Tyson said that on his way to the ring. I keep thinking today is yesterday. Everything went according to plan, my head on the pillow.

*Factory*

They file into the windowless building and vanish from the world as if they had slipped under barbed wire fences under cover of night or been taken away in black, unmarked cars. At noon, the whistle blows and the big box flings open and the Lazaruses pour out, staring straight into the sun with frozen eyes.

## Cardinal

Put me among the old,
I am one of the slow ones,
lost in my days, letting you
cut my meat, drape a sweater
around my shoulders. Place me
among the racers, I cross the line,
arms upraised, my mouth agape.
Lovelorn, I perch on the bridge's rail,
the bay shivers, welcoming my leap.
A radiant dancer, my feet are sore,
my back aches. Place me among
the snow-brushed branches. I am
a bird, watching you from the tree.
You are at the breakfast table,
wearing your robe, lifting a spoon
to your waiting mouth that is tired,
so tired, of words. Look up, high up!

## Legend Two

A poor man in a long, gray coat
To whom much harm, failure, and insult
Have happened upon, walks and walks

Down cobbled streets, through alpine paths,
Across drought-cracked fields and boulevards,
Ashen and overheated, rasping for breath.

His bronchia are horribly infected. To the domestics
And the seamstresses, the plowmen and the beggars,
He is hero for he has taken in

Their tiredness like a tree's thirsty roots,
Like the distant mountain in the cold clouds,
Like the planet's black earth beneath bare feet.

Sometimes he pauses and lets out the moan
Of a felled beast that drops the hunters to their knees.
Sometimes he closes his eyes for days at a time,

Groping along village walls, tumbling into bushes.
*Kann ich ihnen helfen*? Can I help you,
Asks the boy? No, thank you, he whispers,

But mostly he is mute, hieroglyph, invisible.
Sometimes, when you are sleeping, the poor man stands
Outside your house and counts the beats of your heart.

*Great News, Beneficiary*

You are waiting for the over-crowded bus to arrive. Here it comes now! Step out into a world of sparkling water, smoldering tires, hostile peasants, and loving, weeping – wondrous and fair. Sorrow beckons in her torn evening gown, but you have come so far. You are no longer intrigued. "Come when you're ready," you call out to Sorrow. "We'll set a place for you at the table. The fried chicken is delicious." In the freezing lake, you are hauling off with primal screams and laughter. In the fresh-mown field, you are running in the grass, you are swinging on the swing — hello life goodbye hello life goodbye hello life . . .

*Her, I Want Her*

Everywhere I went I stole something,
sandwiches from kiosks, souvenirs, books, tees,
a cap, nothing terribly expensive like diamonds

or rare paintings. Just stuff I could slip into my pocket
or hold in my hand. I lifted one CD and then another
from all the music stores I entered. Sometimes I would wait

at the door, daring them to catch me. No one ever did.
It was so easy. I was quite the virtuoso. My hands moved with
swift agility, my fingers were long and tapered. I accumulated

a beautiful collection of music and even gave some away
as expensive, appreciated gifts. I was a free and generous soul.
Nothing else I have ever done has compared to that rush.

So where did she go that crazy, bold girl, who had no fear
of consequences, who made her exit out of the doors of the world
like Cleopatra on her barge. I don't remember what I did

to make her go away from me. I needed a job and I don't think
she wanted anything to do with that. She lifted out of me
like a ghost and floated away in her own lithe body

and attached herself to another young life. She left me
covered in fear. I suppose it was time. The years passed
and I almost forgot that she ever existed. I wonder

if she got hooked on drugs or took up with the wrong other
and got hurt in terrible ways. Maybe she threw her energy
into a small boat and rode out into the timeless ocean

to rescue dolphins trapped in a net. Set free, the gleaming
dolphins would go out and come back, go out and come back,
and, one day, they came back and seemed to say good bye.

Isis

*She Is*

Pull me down with you, muse, use me, abuse me,
let the frozen pond inside me crack, let me fall through.

I will follow you to the depths where strange, one-eyed creatures
breathe. I hardly exist as flesh and blood among them.

Wounded by their voices, I bring messages back from the realm,
but I am just the instrument playing. She is deep down music.

*I Almost Forgot You Ever Existed*

it was in sacramento or san francisco
and the lauras were there
laura of the aqua eyes
umbrella for shade laura
reeling to laura nyro laura
saint laura of the broken stems
mama's girl laura who ran away bruised
nailed shut laura with her sticky cello
this is a day when I feel not to be alive again laura
naked laura on the street and the cops chasing after
I almost forgot you ever existed laura
tell me you lived happily after
tell me you *lived*

## Avalanche

The whole world could collapse around you

You'd be safe inside

Scooping out snow with bare fists

Inside there is air and there is warmth

If only you had a table and a chair

You hear muffled voices in strange tongues

But you have no desire to make a sound

You are done with desire

Nor do you hunger or thirst

You hear a dog barking and scratching above you

Scratching as at a manhole cover

It must be night

The digging and the scratching

The foot stomping have stopped

And the sweet dog barking once twice

*Three Chords*

Madame Athena, boardwalk fortune-teller, wore a cheap wig and fake gems on every finger.
Outside her run-down booth, a boy in a white shirt and bow tie sawed at the strings of a frozen
violin. It was winter and the child was thin. He seemed frightened, but perhaps he was just cold.
A paper cup sat at his feet. He was probably her grandson or a child she used to beg for her.
I wonder what has become of them. She is certainly gone forever, but he may be a grown man
by now. With what rancor must he think of his childhood on that boardwalk — but I could be
wrong here. She might have been the only warm love he needed to grow into a lovable,
resilient man. Perhaps it is me he remembers with resentment or fantasy, a child myself,
going to a palmist on a dare, my golden slippers, my fur-lined coat, my pockets of easy cash.
Of course, it is possible that I meant nothing to them at all, but here is their poem, the old
fortune-teller on the boardwalk and her musical little boy.

# Selected Poems from
## *Saint Torch*

## The Sadness of Clothes

When someone dies, the clothes are so sad. They have outlived
their usefulness and cannot get warm and full.
You talk to the clothes and explain that he is not coming back

as when he showed up immaculately dressed in slacks and plaid jacket
and had that beautiful smile on and you'd talk.
You'd go to get something and come back and he'd be gone.

You explain death to the clothes like that dream.
You tell them how much you miss the spouse
and how much you miss the pet with its little winter sweater.

You tell the worn raincoat that if you talk about it,
you will finally let grief out. The ancients forged the words
for battle and victory onto their shields and then they went out

and fought to the last breath. Words have that kind of power
you remind the clothes that remain in the drawer, arms stubbornly
folded across the chest, or slung across the backs of chairs,

or hanging inside the dark closet. Do with us what you will,
they faintly sigh, as you close the door on them.
He is gone and no one can tell us where.

*Ponies at the South Pole*
   *after a photograph, Scott Expedition, 1912*

They are quieter than quiet. They are colder than cold
can be imagined. They may very well be blind.

Their ears receive the last sensation, a tiny crumble
of nothing. Their oblong heads tilt toward each other.

   *. . . the end cannot be far* writes the bungling,
stubborn man in his battered white tent,

writes suffering, bungling man.

## My Body

The body she needs me now to cut her food and feed her,
to bring the glass of sweet water, never sweeter, to her mouth,
dry and shuttered. Now it unfurls itself as mouth, fish wet
and bird ascendant to a higher branch, with the taste of peaches
on its tongue, and for a moment she is mine again. The body
she needs me to hold her hand in the antiseptic rooms, the pill-clicking
halls, the ill surrounding her with their ugly eyes surrounding her.
Needs me to massage her neck, her legs, her temples so filled with
ancient *agonia*. Her breathing is shallow now, more so than yesterday.
I alone can tell. She needs me to call her back. She grows evermore
distant, ever deeper, too tired to lift her head, her arms, to speak
the barest of words. I alone know what is happening. The body
she requires me now full force to her kind attention.

*After Dürer*

As when icy illness ends that you never expected
    Could possibly end, and the terrified body, enveloped
In warm water, reposes, you could kiss every child on the hand,
    Every leaf in the forest, every stone of the wall. A low moan escapes
The mouth. Melancholia, the accompanying spirit, is departing with
    Her ratty wings and crusted eyes, her suitcase of rocks.
A shy, small creature steps trembling from the brush.

*At the Burning of Saint Torch*

In my father's fields, tired hands spread manure,
owlets scream in their nests, scaring the children

with the sounds of their wild lives, and the great,
patient oxen pull, pull . . .

A path is being cut through the throng for my cart
and the dancing bear with a ring through its soft nose.

His beautiful fur is wet and glistening.
I enter the delirium like a child enters the playroom,

deaf to the surface of things.
With your last body, pray for the beasts,

to be yoked together with them, to stumble
with them, to be halted, to be rested.

*Goya's Mirth*

1.

Can you hear them shrieking, the filthy witch and the crackly-
skinned insect, slurping bread soup and rising from the table of crusted
        ladles
to dance, damn it, leaping in midair, kicking grief in the fat gut.

2.

Who stinks here?
It is I, Lord, reeling under these heavy, misshapen clothes.
The world waves a fan in front of its nose.
It is the cancer, it is the dying off. It is I, your foul, offensive lady,
your mossy rock. I have a need to stop it, but I cannot.

3.

Push your cart up and down the street. No one sees you, mémère, but you are
        safe here
in Francisco's wild drawing. Forget the words, forget the worms. A dog scrap
        rolls under
the table, forgotten. The dog? You will lie with him soon.

## The Laundry Room

Something about the woman
Who never speaks. The slow movements
As if in a trance, the awareness of me

Behind her, moving forward with my basket of clothes.
This is no longer the dull, pleasant
Laundry room in the newly painted gray

Basement. This is unchangeable time.
Holding the underwear and blackened
Socks, she has relinquished the one

Her heart has been waiting for.
You can see that she held out for a long spell,
Letting a smile pass through her narrow lips

At the supermarket, at the pharmacy,
Where she picked up her headache pills, her
Special soaps for sensitive skin,

Dreaming of warm people,
Some naked, some in flowing caftans,
Walking about on beautiful legs.

*The Letters of Emma Hauck*\*

Come the labyrinth,
come the curdling word, the black ladder,
that tears a hole through the asylum's roof,

troposphere, stratosphere, to make for us
our own anesthesia, lullaby-and-goodnight,
sweet love. Pleased to wear rags around the mouth

and nose to contain the last essence from seeping,
weighted down by gauze, just barely, to keep
us here, by what kind of what.

\*Emma Hauck was committed in 1909 Germany for schizophrenia. She wrote many letters to her husband, saying only, "Sweetheart, come," thousands of times. None were ever delivered. Her letters are now famous examples of "outsider" art.

*Legend*

They will come in a little boat when it is all over
and we are disappeared from this earth, this blessed lighthouse,
to find our winter coats on their pegs and dinner plates washed
and neatly stacked, beds made, one chair at the table tumbled over
in haste, they will surmise, as *man overboard* caused one of us to rush
outside and be swallowed up with the others. The crate of thick rope
unraveled down below so, yes, they will say, it was the tide, a freak wave,
brutal and sudden and stunning as all misfortune, that swept our bodies away,
never to surface, for a hundred years. They swear they can hear us moan
out in the dark, unfathomable waters, as they hurry to where they are going.
They say we are become creatures, with our faces blanked out,
our mouths opening and closing like fish, our skin replaced by brine;
but we are lightsmen, masters of tides, of ropes, of winter coats
and lighthouse loneliness and here is what happened to us:
death came with the sound of ten thousand horses galloping,
breaking down the wall, and chatterbox, confessional Ducat
went quiet and McCarthy and I were crying.

*Snow Diary/1846*

Father saw thin tracks and followed them but found only wild, fleet deer
leaping majestically out of the mounds . . .

Brother heaves the axe more than anything else with such beauty . . .

Huge birds with wings ten feet across soared above our heads and melted
      into the milk-white
sky. Would I were a bird with wings to get about! . . .

The mules fall head first into the drifts and are too tired to get up. Our
      fathers yoke themselves
to each other and lash themselves to the heaped pallets which they pull
      like bullocks . . .

All our eyes are turning blue . . .

We are close, we are close, I say to my friends, who, dark and dumb, can
      no longer . . .

I tumble into California and place my feet slowly, methodically, in the
      right way
so that I might seem a bright young thing again . . .

I am to marry a good man and live in the golden, sumptuous sun that sings
      a mid-stream, that
sings a full tilt without my once done asking . . .

O, my lost ones, days no one knows when the weakness comes over me . . .

*Iktsuarpok**

to rise
from the bed
to go into
the cold
to wait for
the one
who does
not come

to hear
the snow
squeal
beneath
your feet
to see
your breath
fume
to feel
your heart
beat
to look
left
then right
for the one
who is
coming
who does
not come

to sit at
the table
to stare
at the door
for the
one
who is
coming
who does
not come

to go far
far
into
the dark rock
to go deep
deep
into
the cold sea
to look for
the one
who does
not come

*The poem is an interpretation of this single Inuit word.

## On Robert Walser

You saw a dwarf and imagined yourself dwarf
or the old, homeless hag, pushing her cart of junk.

You closed your eyes for days at a time,
groping along the village walls, tumbling into bushes
with an embarrassed gasp.

You adored the gentlewoman in her riding habit
and the chattering birds with faces like walnuts
and feet like twigs, so alive, alert, and active

in their birdie pursuits. Standing alone in your stale,
furnished room, you felt a shudder of feather
and the glowing air grew full, so close. To be alive

was wonderful, but *to be small and to stay small --*
drop of water into the water.

## Inventory of the Royal War Paintings

The warm piss in a dead ear.
The hamstring stretch of a leg

twisted under her, the strung hands
going numb. The fleeing girl's

seared flesh, the shamed faces
turned away from us with grief

in their necks' pulsing cords.
Muzzle the scurvy dogs! the soldier

shrieks, up to his knees in muck.
From the glacial, muttering fields,

here comes cretinous Death
in his grinning black-cat mask,

riding a flying, red-plumed horse.
Catapults arch like vultures.

*Ikon*

Her downcast face is etched in the bread
By the toaster's black char. Her son, pulled down

From his agony on Earth, lives in the shower mold,
On a dog's rump, banana peel, rotting tree stump.

Locked inside these strange bodies, they bring comfort
To the frightened, the going-blind, who line up to touch

Their enormous, broken eyes; their exhausted, empty mouths.
Behold, Mary, your child rides piggy-back, washing ashore

On the skin of a dead squid, crossing the dew-slicked
Meadow on the carapace of a little turtle.

*Théâtre de l'Odéon*

I could not rise from the dark and go out into the cool,
night air of that beautiful city,

could not get on with my conniving, young life.
What had been smooth and good became impossible, slowly,

meticulously, placing one foot in front of the next,
so that legs, as if buried in snow, might inch along the river

and the alleys with the clochards and the cats,
and I might seem a bright young thing again.

All this before the shock of loss, the dying, who linger
with their weak bodies and blank faces,

and my own stupid share of human harm
inflicted upon the innocent,

and long before Time, that asp,
started laughing, *laughing* at me.

*Terminus*

We take buses everywhere together, careful to retrieve
what is left behind. Our stale room fills with abundance:

hats of all sizes, a fine silk scarf, books with curious marginalia,
black umbrellas, eyeglasses for the near- and farsighted,

and even a gray parrot tethered to a stick. *Hello, darling,
how was your day*, he calls out to us, when we come home

from our chores at the immaculate glass hotel. We sip hot
coffee from thick white saucers while sitting on the porch.

We pray for the lost, when the wind rattles the windows
or a big-bellied plane lifts the rows of silent people

into the night sky. We rise with the sun from our warm,
soft beds. *Let's eat corn*, our pretty boy sings.

*Boardwalk in Winter*

The arcade paranoiac hoists a trophy of pulled-out
      roots above his feverish head.
The shaved monkey braves hunger and the wind

      for the gloved hand's stroke.
The child performer in his starched white shirt
      hacks at the strings of a frozen mandolin.

Bald Athena, shivering psychic, has a tooth that needs
      pulling and hammer toes in pink slippers.
She stows her rusty crown and files her nails grown wild.

*the dark tree, the cold sea*

although I know you can never be found
although I know that from the highest height
you cannot be seen you are not hiding
from me or are you is it how you look now
or maybe how I look now all these years gone by
places seen people met not knowing at any time
who I was or how others saw me or did not see me
and how are you wherever you are if I write you a letter
I'll get no answer if I cry out to you to come in my final
hour you will not come but I will still look for you

Selected Poems from
*Hostage*

## Nemesis

The old men with too much gamble in them, whose eyes

Are at peace only when all is lost, see the Queen's quiet face

On the deck of cards, the red cuff of her cloak, the raw tip

Of her tongue, the blood on her dress . . . What fled from them

In their frenzies comes tiptoeing back, choiring, to the marble

Concert hall where Nemesis, in velvet opera cape, is beginning

Her recitative: *it is your turn to go slowly now, with hands*

*clasped behind your back, drowsy from the earth's sweet*

*abundance and her great deprivations, the rows of crooked trees,*

*the streets' bright monotony, to gather up the starving . . .*

## Bach Fugue

Frees the horses from their mechanical bolts,
Keeps the fire from spreading to the sleepers' floor.
The miming dancers in the wings (*swell to great*)
Begin their sly whisperings, their tired arms
Around each other's waist. The old woman spoons yellow cake
Into her (*celestial tremulous*) mouth. Is capable of putting
Poor Gloucester's eyes, glistening, back. Catches the jumpers
With invisible nets from their sad, night bridges;
Finds all those who have been lost to you. The great
Chords, once struck, can never decay.

*Horsehead at a Parisian Fair*

You are still in your face
Where the sun warms your mouth that once bit a mare's
In death-defying pursuit
In the memory of your standing, your fetlocks
Flecked with gold and white
At the flies that arrive full force to gnaw on you
You could almost toss your mane
Much as you would like to move, you look back at everything
In your path with glassy eyes, the mind of a quadriplegic
And of all that is captive
When you died, they placed you on your side
And bent your legs for running

*Kyrie*

The goal posts are off-kilter and the moon slides into my shoes.
I could disappear into the night like a hitcher,
Firebird of cinders,
Lost dogs, rising from their urine-soaked bedding
To await their human names.

In the dark cells, Beato Angelico's angels stream,
Spirals of pure solace, iodine weavings;
And the shining bodies draped in cloth,
Hands and feet missing, are
Feeling the dance in their mouths.

## 19 Chopin Waltzes

Snow falls from rafters of pink, swollen clouds;
moonlight drenches the peasants' fields.

The feathered flesh of a fish, the juice of a peach,
the silver rivers before we named them with color.

All the begetting: the weak limbs and soft bellies,
the faces elongated like the devil himself. The devil

himself! The ship that sails to dreams of Achilles,
the palace of the deaf, the murmuring in centuries' rooms,

the crying of turtle doves, the fleet-footed dancing.
On Earth as in heaven, beauty without reason.

## The Blind Are Sleeping

Their heads tilt gently on the pillows of the field.
Their hands, gesturing at the out-of-sight

with inexhaustible fingers, rest still as cats—
self-contained, melancholy—beside their prone masters.

The emptied body accommodates the most mottled flesh,
the most hapless limp. The blood that stops is rich

and tender. The aroma of wet grass and turf upturned
is the odor of young men, flavor of salt storm, of shout.

The sun still above is huge and boiling. The heads of the blind
warm like stones, their pale stares mesmerized, forever entering.

Their faces, unadorned, are devoid of human adoration.
Their mouths part as if they could almost sing.

*Let me breathe you*, says the choirmaster, who paints eyes
on their lids, and the blind who sleep—fly out.

*Beast of Burden*

piled so high the legs buckle
hit with a thin stick whistled at
shouted at kicked with their heels

end me
on this earth with these humans
under a boiling sun with rocks

remove the tower of wooden collar
studded with bells
from round my thick neck
so that removed
from all halters I may wander

let the dust blow me away
to long quiet roads
the clip clop of my feet
the only music I hear

or let me be gently lead like the old
or pull the wooden cart of babies
and nothing more

Lord of the Ass
lay me down
unencumbered in your green pastures
for which they incessantly pray

the air cooling and petting the bones of my ears
brushing my skull
the still waters washing out
my braying mouth

## Kafka's Sister

. . . but here is my Ottla, so alive inside her dressing gown,
her breasts like lady apples. See how she bends to pick up
Puss 'n Boots and bring him to her mouth, kissing him
on the rump! (That I were that cat!) How funny she finds me,
seated in my straight-backed chair, fastidious in overcoat,
gloves and bowler hat. "You look like you've seen a ghost,"
she is laughing. "So Franz!" Banished from my kingdom,
all icy winter and future's grief, now that she is here, her
dark hair falling down and around her face and the animal.

*Away*

The faint, hoarse breathing of a near-ghost sliding her arms
into a coat's listless sleeves. Just where does she think she is going in
that mothy thing, with a filthy stray shoved into the pocket, mumbling,
casting elephant shadows along the black walls of blind alleys,
crumbling buildings, a padlocked lumber yard, the dump,
and farther out, the red-lit hut with psychic inside, until
where, on the edge of the dark city, nothing more is.

## Silent Movie

Suddenly all the pedestrians and street vendors are
actors in the new silent movie: *The Horse that Stole
Our Hearts and Galloped Off the Cliff, Its Iron Hooves
Pawing.* Quickly, by the North Gate, for the city
is in flames and we will all perish! The horses are pulled
by ropes round their necks. The old grip tree trunks.
The newly arrived from dung-filled lands are grabbing up
cheap wool gloves, rubber boots, golden doorknobs
and going with hands clenched. Gap-toothed women
squeeze every cherry in the box with swift, nimble fingers.

*Harvest*

A woman with huge ears is stirring a kettle with a shovel
while out in the endless fields girls in gray bonnets and aprons

strain for hours to shake branches down. Fruit is bruised; the dredging
of water pots over blistered shoulders to the plowmen with restless hands

and someone is always being whipped, always being entered. So many children
in rough clothes, chasing the chickens, the pigs, the yoked oxen,

the tethered birds, the wide-eyed donkey with his birch bundles
and pulled logs. A sword disappears and reappears from out of a dark mouth,

a snake is charmed, a boy's body sways with the fever of the bloodied palms.
In the yellow fields, the lute, the lyre, the sweet pipes. Two figures

in red hats, until the trees erase them. Someone being bedded
in cool white sheets, someone dark-crowning from between

long legs, someone blowing on the soup. Loose bodies are sinking
into the sod, the skin sloughing off her beautiful face, the bothered bones

assembling. The fisherman sitting in the quiet and the fish gasping
next to him. The end of the story is the end of expectation: the door

that stays closed, the sound of shatter, a rush past, a cough, silence.

*While You Slept*

The crows with a soft, astonished flush,
lift from their branches, as no living thing without wings

can get about. There was a great fire
in the city while you slept: fire engines, hoses,

torrential gushes of water looped through open
smoking windows. From the roof, screams and hands

reaching up and down. Ladders all the way to heaven
as one at a time bodies were lowered and others

remained. Someone hurled himself like a mounted acrobat
from a ledge into the empty air. Sirens wailed in the distance.

*For Helen*

The sun shines on your hospital-white gown and your bare feet.
The ground beneath you is bone-dry and filled with rocks. You pay no mind.

All the wounds have healed, the rages calmed and inconsequential
In this bright light of summer. The fatal moments of terror,

The noise of the crowd pressing close to see you, to fork round your high,
Supple body, does not disturb your gravity. It has taken so long

For your clenched fist to open, and now it is hugely bloomed,
Its fingers pointing to the hidden floor where children are filing through

In silent commotion. They could be going to the cool, sparkling
Horse's Spring, for all they know, each holding the shoulder of the next,

A tiny train of shy, amazed souls, their bare feet like yours
Not making a sound. You call out to them, in tender words new minted.

*The Last Circus on Earth*

At the last circus on Earth, papier-mâché parrots are strapped
To each child's wrist. A human elephant with a broken back, one man in front,
One in the back, makes a jaunty, grand entrance to the faint roar of the crowd.

Les Frères Mahoudeau, who have spent each entire morning mending
Their tattered tights, ballet slippers and net, for nothing but this matters,
Are making their tremulous way up the rope ladder.

The night watchman has cut loose the bear with a chained ring through its snout,
And the plumed, trick poodles, and run away with the woman who gets sawed
In half. The stuporous contortionist drowses inside the clown's yellow barrel.

*Quartet for the End of Time*

The pianist's hands hover, await the vanishing
That will break over their heads like a flowering grief.
The tears will not be sewn together, as one by one . . .
Never could they, half-mad, imagine the aloof,
The drowning, gathered inside the burying wave.

*Insomnia*

Here comes the sweeper of the square
With his dry, straw broom, and even the scuttling rats
And the pigeons, with their insatiable bellies,
Their ravenous mouths, have a place to go.
Every gold and crimson Mary holds her son,
Nesting, with his old man's face, thin lips and sharp nipples
On a pale chest. Even the chained lie down in the dark;
Soldiers, sick of shoveling muck and trench, dream of resting
Beneath blankets of snow. The herder grips tight the squirming
Sheep and shears it down to its pink, quivering skin.

*Company*

I've lost my stately others and now there is me with neck
erect and solemn, tightened face. Sometimes I feel they are
peering out from behind white curtains, clutching with long

arthritic fingers the edges of chenille, wiping their mouths
as after a succulent roast or giggling like ninnies in the pantry.
Once I turned, but it was only a wisp of my own dark hair.

I wanted them gone for so long, world devised of nothing
but me, distractionless, pure, but I was wrong. Me is empty
as wilderness, air – no monarchs, no moths.

*The Cellar*

Under the locked grille, the animals are crying.

You hear them while you wait and when the bus pulls up,

Finally, and you get on. That was years ago. The cellar

Is given over to new shopkeepers, one after the other,

Who fail and are replaced. Even the selfish brother,

The crazed neighbor, the criminal in his cell, face of blue

Tattoos, has never allowed a living thing to starve

As you have. Who knows this except for you and the laughing

African with his padlock teeth and flashing gold key.

*Hostage*
  *for W. S. Merwin*

God is in the dogs
The one who turns in circles, the one
With scabs, the one who wears the collar
Who stares and stares
And tries in spite of it to smell the dirt and grass
In the abandonment, torrential muteness
My knees loosened, my glassy eyes of crystals warmed
And it was given
Even should we sleep
Turn weep recite, screaming, "the city is conquered and the little king
Will have to go," insane and unreachable
We are still here

*Notre-Dame de Paris*

What gusts of raw, mad emotion, of unbearable expectation, in this world-cutting-loose of the bells. A crucifix, fashioned of twigs, is being held up to all the draculas, who, convulsed, are going up in smoke to a shriek. Quaking birds are calling for assembly and their plaintive crying is being carried over the voice of the gun. Now the dead are stepping out of their wet shoes, and loosened from their withered chords, are calling to us from the deck of their boat: *Bon voyage, mes chers*! We are beside ourselves: *in ekstasis!*

## Lazarus, Come Out

The sisters are wailing, quite beside themselves with something new.
The pale Christ, lanky as a long-distance runner, seems half-amazed at
what he has done. Sitting up, the awakened one sees the immobile

face of the woman he mounted like a maniac, his body erupting in fever,
in abscess, for want of her, and is indifferent. He can hear the murmurs,
the jeers and coarse laughter on the roads and in the homes, the crush

of a slapped face, the unhinged bells, the dangerous, sullen gaps.
Suddenly visible are the closed faces of the doomers and the open faces
of the doomed, although he is a dark room, his tongue black and stiff.

Fanatics who worship the sun sever their arms as offerings
to help it rise; it rises, and the disinterred one, for a time, continues,
dancing by himself like a horse with its screaming, high-tossing head.

## Apollo's Kiss

Devise Cassandra. Become her, in possession,
And the world becomes perfect. For even gods
Crave perfection. Desire her like a man
And like a man be refused in all your desire.
Surrender: beg a first and last kiss and pray
She will acquiesce, her virtue stirred.
Then, breathe into her mouth the powered
Prophecy and for all you are losing
—the deprivation she will give and give—
Release her half gifted, as you are, half mortal.

In the courtyard, animals are captured
By their hind legs, held up on haunches,
Throats slashed. She walks on burning
Stones. Swift, it is slaughtering season.

[*Exit, Pursued By A Bear.*

The callous henchman is the one devoured, the baby saved.
The wind picks up and sends the lazy dove-sails flying over waves

without a finger raised. Even the starved mongrel, abandoned
by your brother, pries open the ash can with its dirty snout

and finds a roasted chicken sitting right on top. Old-timers, every limb
aching to be straightened, march like pins. The torn angels are being fitted

for new gowns by the seamstress with cold lips. Turn, she mumbles. Turn,
the lovelies. The sun is granting her people a golden day, for no earthly reason.

*Chernobyl*

Crossing in the wrong direction, we are quickly
Sealed off, directionless, earth's blind villagers.
We follow the leader and the riverbank to its dried-out
Roots, while at the merest ruffle of wind, bird, leaf,
We hide ourselves behind the thick bodies of old trees
That have the tiny, sad eyes and the long, delicate lashes
Of chained elephants.  We witness the quiet lives
Of fireflies, igniting themselves, their enviable wings;
The languorous butterfly climbing into the flower's face;
And begin to be muted by our arrival at the inconceivable
Door as when the radiated wolves crept into the hunters'
Huts to be comforted and were comforted.

*Host*

There are two worlds I know of:
the vast illumined
and the
place where I am.

I need the other
the way a virus
needs a host,
but the strange,
loving sisters
hold up their hands.

And my body—
uninhabited—
suffers and wonders:
Whose hands are these?
Whose hair?

## Glenn Gould, Dead at 50

It is darker where I am.
I cannot tell, holding my hand
over one eye, if it is female there.

At six,
I multiplied endlessly
and began to feel close
to sacrifice.

The music took root
inside, like torture,
all tension, ritard, release.

It is in every part
of my body now, and there is not
room left for me.

I have burned
all my capes, got rid of my papers.

## The Scarlatti Sun

The mute seamstress on her knees
sticks a pin in the hem
and weeps for the cloth;

the dead stop their dying,
their heads warming like stones in
the Scarlatti sun,

while the grave postman,
his worn leather bag strapped to his back,
feels his mind go, windswept.

An old woman at her window,
her old cat on the sill, sips thick coffee
from a saucer, and in the shuttered convent,

the novitiate, taken up,
rushes across the just-washed floor,
daring the ground to break a bone.

## Acknowledgements

The author wishes to thank the editors of the following publications where these poems originally appeared.

### I

*Agni*: "A Dream Called Us"
*The Harvard Review*: "Nihil" and "You Have Devoured Everything"
*The Paris Review*: "The Suicide of Cesare Pavese"
*Poetry*: "Taming the Parakeet" and "Unrest"
*The Yale Review*: "Trumpet"

### II

*The Denver Quarterly*: "Terminus"
*Five Points, Journal of Literature & Art*: "Goya's Mirth" and "The Laundry Room"
*The Harvard Review*: "Théâtre de l'Odéon"
*The Massachusetts Review*: "My Body" and "Iktsuarpok"
*MiPOesias*: "The Letters of Emma Hauck"
*The New Republic*: "Ponies at the South Pole"
*Ploughshares*: "After Dürer"
*Poem-A-Day/Academy of American Poets*: "the dark tree, the cold sea" and "The Sadness of Clothes"
*The Threepenny Review*: "On Robert Walser"
*The Yale Review*: "Inventory of the Royal War Paintings"
"The Sadness of Clothes" appeared In *The Best American Poetry, 2016*, editor, Edward Hirsch
"After Dürer" appeared in the anthology, *Poems of Gratitude*, The Everyman's Pocket Library
"Boardwalk in Winter" appeared in the anthology, *The Traveler's Vade Mecum*

### III

*The American Poetry Review*: "Lazarus, Come Out" and "Silent Movie"
*The Boston Review*: "Chernobyl"

*Chelsea*: "Apollo's Kiss"

*The Cimarron Review*: "Insomnia" and "19 Chopin Waltzes"

Columbia: *Journal of Literature*: "The Blind Are Sleeping"

*The New Yorker*: "Bach Fugue"

*The Paris Review:* "Company"

*Parnassus:* "The Scarlatti Sun"

*Ploughshares*: "Hostage"

*Poetry:* "Nemesis" and "The Cellar"

*The Yale Review:* "Harvest"

"Apollo's Kiss" appeared in *The Best American Poetry, 1998*, editor, John Hollander

"Bach Fugue" appeared in the anthology, *Music's Spell*, The Everyman's Pocket Library

"19 Chopin Waltzes" appeared in the anthology, *Chopin with Cherries*

"Glenn Gould, Dead at 50" appeared in the anthology, *Northern Music*, John G. Burke Publisher, Inc., and was reprinted in Piano/*International Piano*, 2002

"Nemesis" and "19 Chopin Waltzes" and "The Cellar" were reprinted in *Verse Daily*

"Nemesis" was reprinted in *The Columbia Granger's World of Poetry*

**Notes**

"You have devoured everything" is a line from a letter of Honoré de Balzac.

"Quartet for the End of Time" was composed by Olivier Messiaen.

"[Exit, Pursued By A Bear." is a famous stage direction from Shakespeare's *The Winter's Tale*.

Sincere appreciation and thank you to Diana Schultz and Greg Miller for their excellent work on my Sheep Meadow books. Finally, a special thank you to Stanley Moss for his loving support of me and my poetry and for making this book possible.